YOUR
Ramadan
JOURNAL

YOUR
Ramadan
JOURNAL

Embrace Your Spirituality
and Rediscover Your
Purpose

HUMZA KHAN

Illustrated by
Amirah Sheikh and
Hope Lione

Michael O'Mara Books Limited

Thank you to my mother for her words of wisdom throughout the writing process. I am humbled to have written this journal and hope it is of benefit to readers; not just through Ramadan, but beyond the holy month. All praises be to Allah (SWT). All good that has come from writing this journal is from Him; any mistakes are mine and I pray that He forgives me if any are made. Ameen.

First published in Great Britain in 2024 by
Michael O'Mara Books Limited
9 Lion Yard
Tremadoc Road
London SW4 7NQ

A CIP catalogue record for this book is available from the British Library.

Papers used by Michael O'Mara Books Limited are natural, recyclable products made from wood grown in sustainable forests. The manufacturing processes conform to the environmental regulations of the country of origin.

ISBN: 978-1-78929-679-2 in paperback print format

1 2 3 4 5 6 7 8 9 10

Illustrations by Amirah Sheikh and Hope Lione
Cover design by Natasha Le Coultre, using an illustration by Amirah Sheikh and Hope Lione
Designed by Barbara Ward and Claire Cater

Printed and bound in China

www.mombooks.com

CONTENTS

INTRODUCTION

In the name of God – the Most Beneficent, Most Merciful.

Ramadan is the ninth month of the Islamic (Hijri) calendar and is the holiest month for Muslims, as it involves fulfilling one of the five pillars of Islam. It is a command by Allah (*Subhanahu Wa Ta'ala, Most Glorious, the Exalted*) for those with ability and capacity to do so. We fast from sunrise to sunset, and it eclipses abstinence from food and drink, as it is an opportunity to rekindle worship with Him through closeness and connection.

'Ramadan is the month in which the Qur'an was revealed as a guide for humanity with clear proofs of guidance and the decisive authority. So, whoever is present this month, let them fast. But whoever is ill or on a journey, then (let them fast) an equal number of days (after Ramadan). Allah intends ease for you, not hardship, so you may complete the prescribed period and proclaim the greatness of Allah for guiding you, and perhaps you will be grateful.' (Qur'an, 2:185).

This journal is an opportunity for you to connect with your faith during this beautiful month and work towards living your life consistent with Islamic values and beliefs. The act of fasting is not only a core tenant of worship, but has numerous benefits for us spiritually, physically and psychologically.

What is unique about this journal is that it uses mindfulness exercises to give space to explore Islamic concepts and its connection with or relevance to our *deen* (religion/way of life), and shows you how to strengthen your relationship with the All-Mighty, with yourself and others in your life. Modernity has become saturated with overwhelming distractions and stressors. As this can impact how we experience Ramadan, we encourage a digital detox and the use of pen on paper, as this has shown to have many benefits, from improved mood and health to increased creativity and mastery of self.

The journal is divided into three sections: the first part looks at what we can do as we come to approach the holy month of Ramadan; the second looks at what we can do *during* the holy month; the third will look at what we can take from the month and incorporate into our lives. Most importantly, I want to be able to show you how to take subtle, practical steps and integrate them into your day-to-day living, and work towards being a better Muslim, *Insha'Allah* (God willing).

Humza Khan

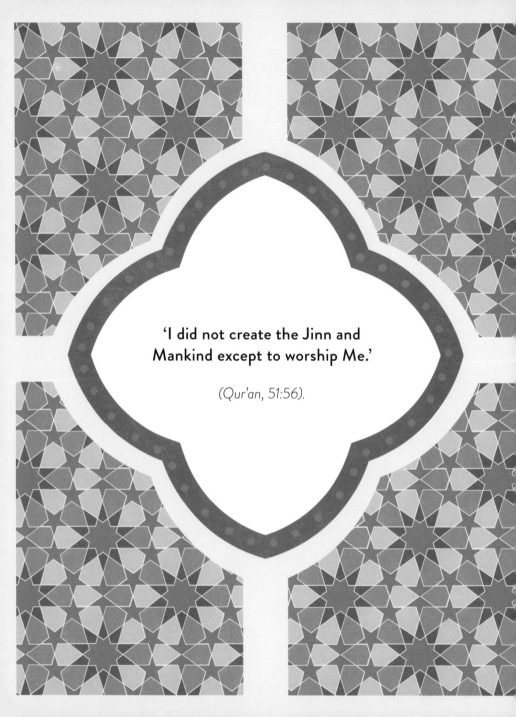

'I did not create the Jinn and Mankind except to worship Me.'

(Qur'an, 51:56).

PREPARING FOR RAMADAN

As Ramadan nears, it is imperative that we – as observant Muslims – are mindful of what we are about to embark on. This sets a healthy precedence for the month itself. But what do we do beyond the act of abstaining from food and water? In this section, I'd like you to think about considerations as the month approaches and then take gentle steps towards building a robust foundation, to ensure that your Ramadan is optimized.

When we create a plan and look forward to scheduled activities, we develop a greater sense of motivation; hence we are more likely to do them. This is because we have greater clarity with what we set out to achieve, which offers us a practical and psychological boost.

The Prophet Muhammad (Peace and Blessings Upon Him) said: 'Whoever fasts Ramadan out of faith and the hope of reward will be forgiven (for previous sins).' (Ibn Majah).

EMBRACE MINDFULNESS

Mindfulness is more than a buzzword; it is a philosophical way of living. It is something we can actively immerse ourselves in and requires us to be able to observe with curiosity and tune into our senses. To be in a state of mindfulness means to stay in the present moment and react without judgement to what you experience.

Becoming more aware of your body and mind is truly empowering when you start to actively recognize what your senses experience or absorb. You may not believe it, but serenity is something you have the capacity for, or already possess, and you can harness it to achieve your goals.

Things I can start paying more attention to, or be curious about

_____

_____

_____

_____

_____

How I found this, noting any differences to how I usually engage in tasks

_____

_____

_____

_____

_____

MINDFULNESS WITHIN ISLAM

During Ramadan, Muslims can practise being present and conscious of God, and remembering Him in all that we do. The practice of *muraqabah* (mindfulness) can help you to develop a connection with Him, as you exercise silence as a means of being closer to the All-Mighty. It is within this space that you will begin to regulate your thoughts and feelings, through a disciplined approach that will cultivate focus and a deeper awareness of the presence of Allah (SWT).

Think about how you can combine *taqwa* (being conscious and cognizant of God) and the concept of mindfulness, considering positive emotions are associated with good physical and mental health, and longevity. 'Know that Allah is aware of what is in your hearts, so be mindful of Him.' (Qur'an, 2:235).

*Ways I can
practise mindfulness with taqwa (an example
may be when you're performing salah (prayer),
preparing food for iftar (meal after sunset/
breaking fast) or while doing wudhu (ablution)*

_____

_____

_____

_____

_____

_____

_____

YOUR FIVE SENSES

How do you begin taking such steps to incorporate mindfulness into your life? Start by being aware of the five senses (sight, smell, sound, touch and taste) and exercising them to attune yourself towards *what* you might be doing, *who* you might be with and *where* you may be.

An overstimulation of our senses can affect our ability to regulate our thoughts and can leave us feeling more overwhelmed. This can have lingering effects on our interactions with others and decrease the quality of our experiences, i.e. while we engage in *dhikr* or prayer.

The benefits of *muraqabah* involve spiritual excellence, which The Messenger (PBUH) narrated 'is to worship Allah as if you see Him, for if you do not see Him, He certainly sees you'. (Bukhari).

1. *Sight. The colours, gradients, textures, composition, tones and details I notice*

_____

_____

_____

2. *Smell. The aromas I notice and how they make me feel*

_____

_____

_____

3. *Sound. The different types of sound I can hear, noting the volume, rhythms, melodies and details*

_____

_____

_____

_____

4. Touch. What I can feel, and what sensations it gives me, noticing the textures, the compositions and the details

_____

_____

_____

5. Taste. What I am consuming and the flavours I can taste, as well as the textures, the tones and the contrasts I notice

_____

_____

_____

_____

_____

How I can mindfully embrace my senses

1. Sight

_____

_____

2. Smell

_____

_____

3. Sound

_____

_____

4. Touch

_____

_____

5. Taste

_____

_____

STARTING GENTLY

Rajab and Shab'an are the seventh and eighth months of the Islamic calendar that precede Ramadan. These opportune months provide fertile ground to harvest and irrigate changes just before the holy month. Having a goal in mind and taking small and gentle steps towards it can help with successfully achieving it.

Ramadan is not merely going through the motions or abstaining from food, water or that which displeases God. It's an opportunity to begin building new and healthy habits or strengthen existing practices. As a result, we want to be mindful of what we are doing and the reasoning behind it, as placing Him at the centre of our lives will feed our motivation.

One way to prepare for Ramadan is to read the Qur'an – even a few pages can help – to ensure that your Arabic reading or comprehension is ready for an entire month of supplication. Another good place to start is by making up for missed fasts from last Ramadan or setting the pace and easing your body through the '*sunnah* (voluntary) fasts' (Mondays and Thursdays) or 'the white days' (13th, 14th and 15th of every Islamic month).

My reasons for Ramadan

_____

_____

_____

What I want to achieve in the holy month

_____

_____

_____

Meaningful ways I can physically and mentally prepare for Ramadan

_____

_____

_____

YOUR VALUES

Understanding why we fast for a month, the purpose it serves and what we hope to gain from it is important when embarking on the journey of Ramadan. It can be helpful for us to think about our values, and what we stand for as Muslims. Our values are a navigation system – like a compass. They function to direct us in a particular way. Before we decide where we want to go, we first need to identify what our values are and what it is about them that enriches our *deen*.

Ask yourself:

- What do you want to do with your time in this *dunya* (world/worldly life)?
- What is important and why?
- What qualities do you want to possess?
- What does Allah (SWT) encourage you to do?
- How might you embody this in practice?

Shared values can bring the *ummah* (nation/community of believers) together, in fostering a sense of community, strengthening spirituality and reaching a robust *deen*. Typical values can include family, authenticity, relationships, spirituality, courage, physical health, community, trust and personal growth.

The things that are important to me

What gives me a sense of purpose

FOCUS ON WHAT YOU
CAN CONTROL

Ramadan is an opportunity to soothe the soul, as we shift our focus away from worries which we cannot control by working towards being present and adhering to the practice of *tawakkul* (placing our trust in God). As you begin to accept Allah's (SWT) plan, commit to focusing on what you can control and conduct yourself in ways that align with your Islamic values.

Making plans to strengthen our *deen* helps increase our chances of attaining our Ramadan goals. It would be like comparing someone going to the supermarket with a shopping list vs without a list – knowing what we want, being efficient with our time and successfully completing tasks.

A few examples can be praying every *sunnah salah*, engaging in daily *adkhar* (remembrance of God), going for afternoon walks, eating *suhoor/iftar* (meal before sunrise/commencing fast) with family or friends or in the community, reflecting on God's plan through journaling, reading the Qur'an in the afternoon after *dhuhr* (midday prayer), and making *du'a* (supplication/invocation) after every *salah*.

My goals for Ramadan

MORNING MEDITATION

A part of mindfulness is to help develop our attention, with curiosity and kindness, in order to have flexibility with how we approach situations or experiences which life brings us. This infuses with self-reflection, as we tap into our inner world and practise being present in sheer silence – away from worldly distractions, including our inner voice.

1. Sit up straight, wherever you may be, as your spine supports itself. You can close your eyes or lower your gaze and put your feet flat on the floor.

2. As you breathe in and out, pay attention to your body's different sensations. Notice your breathing, keeping it as natural as possible.

3. Your mind may wander. If that is the case, let it do so with a gentle curiosity.

4. Your mind may or may not be relaxed and calm. Whatever you observe, allow it to be.

5. A minute later, gently open your eyes and take note of what is around you.

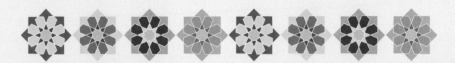

How I can use this meditative activity to ground myself

What I noticed before and afterwards

NEW BEGINNINGS

As Ramadan arrives, think about approaching the month with a clean heart and peace of mind. This is where we can seek forgiveness for our sins – whether for yourself or between you and God and/or others. It is in human nature to err, but how mindful we are of this and how we respond to this is what matters most. The Prophet Muhammad (PBUH) narrated, 'By the One in whose hand is my soul, if you did not sin, Allah would replace you with people who would sin, and they would seek forgiveness from Allah and He would forgive them.' (Muslim).

How I can take steps towards forgiveness (who this involves and what it concerns)

_____

_____

_____

_____

Why I want forgiveness and what it looks like

_____

_____

_____

_____

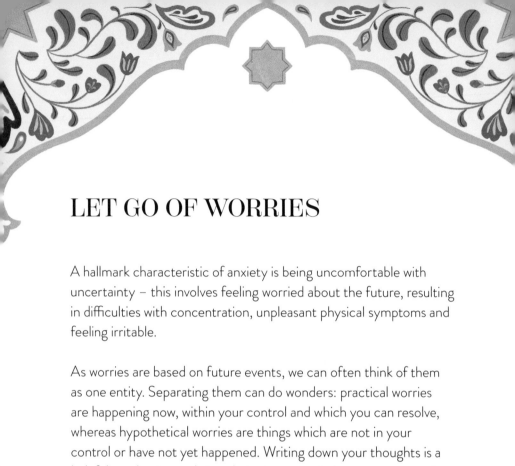

LET GO OF WORRIES

A hallmark characteristic of anxiety is being uncomfortable with uncertainty – this involves feeling worried about the future, resulting in difficulties with concentration, unpleasant physical symptoms and feeling irritable.

As worries are based on future events, we can often think of them as one entity. Separating them can do wonders: practical worries are happening now, within your control and which you can resolve, whereas hypothetical worries are things which are not in your control or have not yet happened. Writing down your thoughts is a helpful mechanism to bring clarity to your mind, as you process the information through the mind of your eye, which offers pause and perspective.

Things I can let go of to start Ramadan in the most peaceful way possible

_____

_____

_____

_____

Are my worries practical or hypothetical? Do I need to deal with them now, is it about something in the future or is it out of my control?

_____

_____

_____

CONTROLLED BREATHING

The act of breathing is governed by the autonomic nervous system. It ought to occur naturally and is one of the easiest and most effective ways to alleviate stress or anxiety. Breathing regulates how we feel because of two systems: sympathetic – breathing in, which is a bit like pressing on the accelerator of a vehicle; and parasympathetic – breathing out, which is like pressing the brakes of a vehicle.

Managing our breathing can provide us with greater levels of self-awareness, which in turn has physical health benefits. If you are feeling overwhelmed, a simple breathing technique is to count each breath (in your head):

1. While taking a slow breath, inhale through your nose.

2. On the long exhale, breathe out through your mouth.

3. On the subsequent inhalations, breathe slowly through your nose.

4. On a final exhale, gently release through your mouth.

How I can practise regulating my breathing in situations of stress and anxiety

_____

_____

_____

_____

_____

How did I find this? What did I notice?

_____

_____

_____

_____

_____

AWARENESS OF GOD

A living component of faith is *shukr* (gratitude). This itself is considered a state of worship, as we consciously seek to become more mindful of, and recognize, the goodness we receive and attribute it to Allah. This represents inward experiences and outward expressions, where *shukr* is felt in the heart and demonstrated through how we behave.

The Messenger (PBUH) narrated, 'I am amazed by the believer. If he is granted goodness, he praises Allah and is grateful. If he is afflicted with a calamity, he praises Allah and is patient.' (Ahmad).

The idea of goodness is anything that brings us closer to Him. It is through *shukr* that we can transform ourselves as individuals, as we become more mindful of our experiences, begin to foster healthier and stronger relationships with others, and cultivate our love for God. This feeds our sense of closeness and connection, which is paramount to our shared existence on earth.

How I can become more mindful of and connect my blessings to Allah's names and attributes

_____

_____

_____

_____

_____

_____

_____

_____

BUILD YOUR COMMUNITY

As we start fasting, it may be worthwhile reflecting on what this means to you or involves for others, as it can be a time of mixed emotions for some. As you prepare for Ramadan, think about how you can build your sense of community and show qualities such as empathy, compassion and understanding.

The Prophet Muhammed (PBUH) said: 'Whoever relieves a Muslim from the burdens of the world, Allah will relieve him of them on the Day of Judgement. Whoever helps ease difficulties in the world, Allah will grant him ease in the world and the hereafter. And whoever covers the faults of a Muslim, Allah will cover his faults in the world and the hereafter. And Allah is engaged in helping His worshippers as long as they are engaged in helping others.' (Tirmidhi).

My community includes

_____

_____

What I value most about these relationships

_____

_____

How I can show compassion and understanding towards others

_____

_____

_____

MOVE YOUR BODY

Despite fasting, having a sense of physical activity throughout the month is essential for wellbeing. People feel calmer, more awake and content after periods of being physically active, compared to after inactivity. Physical movement and exercise are effective ways to help boost our mood.

Movement in any capacity, whether it's in short bursts throughout the day or for a set window of time, can maintain the body's natural rhythm and prevent you from feeling like you are withering away the hours of the blessed month. What kind of activities can you do to move your body and keep your mind active? How present are you during this? What do you notice? A few examples can include going for walks, stretching through yoga, going for a run, as well as resistance training.

Activities which boost my energy and motivation

_____

_____

_____

_____

Ways I can incorporate activity into my day

_____

_____

_____

_____

BE KIND TO YOURSELF

Ramadan is a chance to practise being compassionate. This means listening to your body and respecting that this process is for God. As a result, we want to take measures that ensure the longevity and maximization of our participation in our *deen* during this month.

This could mean hydrating well during *suhoor/iftar*, to managing portions and eating foods which can offer you energy for the day/night, to planning appropriate rest during the day and pacing yourself – such as taking breaks from work or study, including a potential nap. It could mean prioritizing yourself – whether taking annual leave or adjusting work, for example starting later or making subtle changes to your workload.

How I can prepare in advance
for and treat myself with kindness
during Ramadan

_____

_____

_____

_____

_____

_____

_____

POSITIVE SELF-TALK

The mind works in patterns, where if we access one pattern very frequently, it can be more difficult to produce another. This really shapes our inner voice. You can intentionally direct thoughts to yourself which will override negative thought patterns, not only to create a better mindset but also a healthier perspective on life. If you take steps practising compassion, it will not only alleviate stress, but will also help to organize your thoughts and feelings in a more sustainable way.

This is not just for the benefit of our loved ones, but also for ourselves. If you think about compassion, we want to hold it with feelings of gentleness; pay attention to your thoughts with humility, and notice feelings that arise from within. Imagine how you would respond to someone you love or care about, or perhaps how someone who you deeply regard would speak to you.

How I can respond to self-criticism during Ramadan

_____

_____

_____

_____

_____

_____

How did I find this? What did I notice?

_____

_____

_____

_____

_____

_____

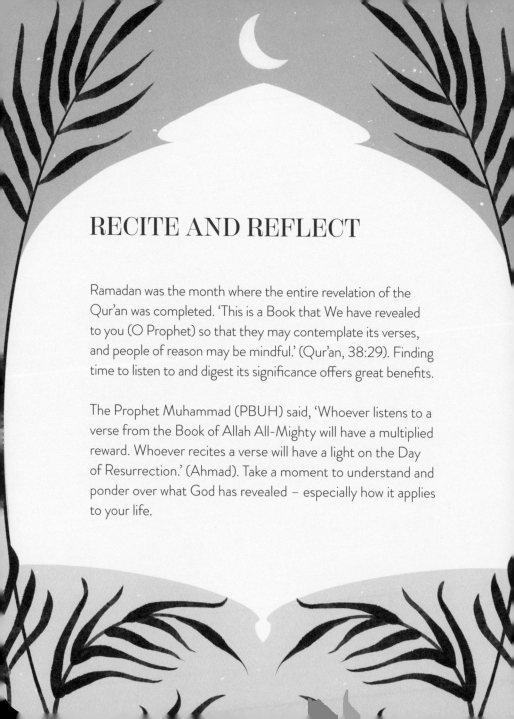

RECITE AND REFLECT

Ramadan was the month where the entire revelation of the Qur'an was completed. 'This is a Book that We have revealed to you (O Prophet) so that they may contemplate its verses, and people of reason may be mindful.' (Qur'an, 38:29). Finding time to listen to and digest its significance offers great benefits.

The Prophet Muhammad (PBUH) said, 'Whoever listens to a verse from the Book of Allah All-Mighty will have a multiplied reward. Whoever recites a verse will have a light on the Day of Resurrection.' (Ahmad). Take a moment to understand and ponder over what God has revealed – especially how it applies to your life.

How I can recite and reflect on what God has revealed to us

_____

_____

_____

_____

_____

Specific surahs (chapters) that I want to understand better

_____

_____

_____

_____

_____

NEW SURAHS

'When the Qur'an is recited, listen to it attentively and be silent, so you may be shown mercy.' (Qur'an, 7:204).

Ramadan provides us with a chance to learn the Qur'an, which Allah affirms as a mechanism of instilling belief in Him, feeding into our *taqwa* and *tawakkul*. This further benefits our *akhirah* (afterlife/ hereafter), as The Prophet Muhammad (PBUH) said, 'Recite the Qur'an, for it will come as an intercessor for its reciters on the Day of Resurrection.' (Muslim).

A profound supplication: 'Our Lord, give us in this world (that which is) good and in there hereafter (that which is) good and protect us from the punishment of the fire.' (Qur'an, 2:201).

New surahs I would like to
study during the month of Ramadan

_____

_____

_____

_____

_____

_____

Surahs that I want to memorize

_____

_____

_____

_____

_____

_____

YOUR RAMADAN ESSENTIALS

As Muslims, Ramadan provides us with moments to contemplate and facilitate essential changes we want to make. It can be helpful to think about this in terms of a spiritual toolkit.

This ranges from but isn't limited to reading the Qur'an passages daily (with *tilawat*, or mindful/reflective recitation), praying *sunnah* (voluntary) before or after *fardh* (obligatory) *salah*, being consistent with praying with a *tasbih* (prayer beads to count *dhikr*) after *salah*, incorporating *du'a* and/or *dhikr*, to giving extra charity, to seeking forgiveness, to being more eco-conscious and reducing waste, to praying *tahajjud* (morning prayer) and more. What will be essential for us in preparation for and during Ramadan will vary from person to person.

'O believers! Always remember Allah often.' (Qur'an, 33:41).

What is most important and relevant to me?

What do I need to prioritize for the holy month? Do I have everything I need for the month ahead?

SET YOUR INTENTIONS

The Prophet Muhammad (PBUH) said, 'Verily, Allah does not look at your appearance or wealth, but rather He looks at your hearts and actions.' (Muslim). The intentions (*niyyah*) we hold before engaging in any act of worship, including our fasts, can determine the success of our Ramadan.

'Say, (O Prophet), "whether you conceal what is in your hearts or reveal it, it is known to Allah. For He knows whatever is in the heavens and whatever is on the earth. And Allah is Most Capable of everything".' (Qur'an, 3:29). Allah knows what is in our hearts, and he sees the foundation towards appreciating Him in times of both hardship and ease. Within Islam, intentions are paramount, as this is iterated before any act of worship, i.e. performing prayers, opening/breaking of the fast, when giving to charity, or performing pilgrimage.

My intentions for Ramadan are to

_____

_____

_____

_____

How I can be mindful of my intentions behind my daily activities or actions

_____

_____

_____

_____

YOUR RAMADAN CALENDAR

In this blessed month, we strive to make a conscious effort to act according to our values and engage in behaviours which nourish our soul. This includes strengthening our relationship to our Maker, connecting with our family and scheduling activities which will make us feel contentment, whether it be striving to pray, reading pages of the Qur'an, helping with preparing for *suhoor/iftar* or volunteering at the local *masjid* (place of worship). What do you schedule for the month of Ramadan? Use the space opposite to create some structure to what you intend to achieve and refer to this throughout the month – balance is essential.

Day 1

Day 2

Day 3

Day 4

Day 5

Day 6

Day 7

Day 8

Day 9

Day 10

Day 11

Day 12

Day 13

Day 14

Day 15

Day 16

Day 17

Day 18

Day 19

Day 20

Day 21

Day 22

Day 23

Day 24

Day 25

Day 26

Day 27

Day 28

Day 29

Day 30

'Remember Me; I will remember you.
And thank Me, and never be ungrateful.'

(Qur'an, 2:152).

YOUR RAMADAN RITUALS

Now we begin to embark on this blessed and auspicious month, we want to be mindful of how we can utilize our time and space to maximize our experiences, i.e. opportunities to gain reward and raise our ranks. This will offer us a clear vision of what we can do to ensure that we gain benefit and feel contentment/closeness to God. This section will cover approaches that we will want to adopt and refine for ourselves, whether daily or at specific moments in the month.

THE FIRST SUHOOR AND IFTAR

The first fast we endure and complete fills us with great excitement but can also equally be challenging. Your sleep will be disrupted, your energy levels dip, and the routine you were previously accustomed to is completely uprooted.

Allowing ourselves distance, to look at the details of our daily existence, can provide perspective. This will begin to feed contentment and *shukr*. As we attribute Allah for the good, we will start to shift the lens through which we view our lives.

The Prophet (PBUH) said, 'Whoever provides food for breaking of the fast for a fasting person receives the reward of the fasting person.' (Tirmidhi and Ibn Majah).

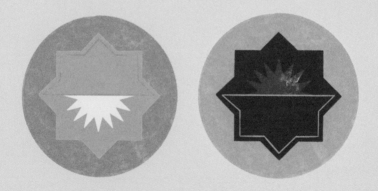

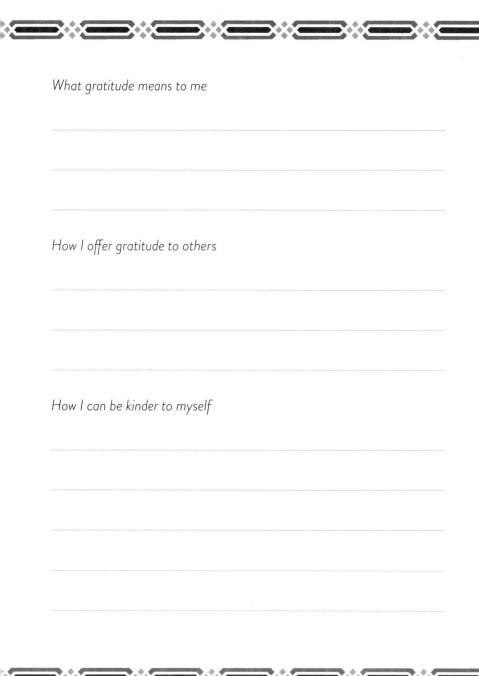

What gratitude means to me

_____

_____

_____

How I offer gratitude to others

_____

_____

_____

How I can be kinder to myself

_____

_____

_____

_____

BODY SCAN MEDITATION

Try incorporating elements of meditation which can be practised away from the prayer mat. We reconnect with our bodies in different atmospheres. When you're feeling overwhelmed, I want you to attempt to scan your body to release this stress – being in the present, regardless of your immediate response to something upsetting or overwhelming, can ground you and provide ease.

Help to develop your ability to fully immerse in and pay attention to the present; this is particularly useful when thoughts or feelings seem chaotic. Taking a more non-judgemental approach allows ourselves the time and space to be at one with ourselves.

1. Close your eyes or lower your gaze to a fixed spot to allow you to focus.

2. Become aware of your breathing, noticing both inhalations and exhalations. Pay attention to the sensation this brings and allow yourself the gentleness that comes with being curious.

3. When you are ready, pay close attention to wherever you would like to explore in your body. This can be done methodically, from the top of your head to the soles of your feet.

4. You may notice a range of sensations, e.g. tightness, stiffness, tingling, pressure, temperature. How does this feel? Do you notice anything else? Identify without judgement.

6. Your mind may wander or drift off to sleep. Merely recognize this as a positive sign, to be fully present in the moment and give your body the place to rest.

7. Slowly bring your attention back to investigating the many feelings in your body – repeat this as many times as you want.

8. Spend a little moment to expand your attention to feeling your entire body in a state of exhalation. And then gently open your eyes and observe your surroundings.

How did I find this? What did I notice?

'Verily, the most honourable of you with Allah is that (believer) who has At-Taqwa. Verily, Allah is All-Knowing, All-Aware.'

(Qur'an, 49:13).

SELF-REFLECTION

Being aware of what is in our heart and mind is an essential ingredient for self-reflection. Ramadan serves as an opportunity for us to foster this quality. Begin by recognizing how you feel, think and behave – the various patterns which permeate your daily life.

Exercising mindfulness will lay the foundations for harnessing your true potential. When you practise recognizing your inner dialogue, and making a choice on what will nurture you, you will feel empowered and become more aligned with your values.

Throughout the day when you're fasting, try to be mindful of and notice your surroundings, such as situations which evoke a feeling or reaction from you, whether positive or negative. Reflecting on your day is a chance to put into perspective our struggles or hardship.

My daily reflections of my experiences and how this makes me feel

FIND YOUR PURPOSE

As we navigate through our days and moments, it is important for us to do things with a purpose. By using our senses to be as present as possible, we are working to build our connection with and understanding of God and His creation.

This is where we want to translate our values into tangible goals that we can achieve. Look back over previous exercises in this journal; as you strive towards finding purpose, seek to address why your purpose is meaningful to you as a Muslim. How can you become closer to them?

One way to guide finding your purpose can be to mindfully practise *dhikr* while reciting the Qur'an, i.e. *tilawat*, doing *wudhu*, as well as helping to prepare for the *iftar* meal, washing the dishes, doing the grocery shop, and more. How can you act more consistently with your values?

Activities/tasks I can do to give me a sense of purpose

_____

_____

_____

_____

_____

How I can undertake these activities with purpose and incorporate them beyond

_____

_____

_____

_____

_____

STAY IN THE MOMENT

As mindfulness helps with discipline, this interweaves with what Ramadan entails; so being aware of the present means grounding ourselves, improving our focus and returning to how we want to align with our values as a practising Muslim.

Have you ever felt like you've strayed away from the straight path? It's normal for our faith to fluctuate and it is common to feel distant or undeserving, or even become distracted by the *dunya*. 'Whenever a surah is revealed, some of them ask "which of you has this increased in faith?" As for the believers, it has increased them in faith and they rejoice.' (Qur'an, 9:124).

Just being present can be challenging, but mindfully acknowledging that is the start of challenging the negative thoughts or feelings which arise. Make the most of being present by showing *shukr* to Allah (SWT), consciously coming closer to the *deen* and giving your life meaning, while connecting with those around you and with whatever you do – nourishing your soul.

*How I refocus my attention
and practise staying in the moment*

PAUSE AND REFLECT

This is a chance to review the goals you set yourself just before Ramadan – how are you getting on with them? Our brains are neuroplastic. This means that they are malleable, and they can change and adapt according to our experiences.

Setting goals is a powerful mechanism to facilitate change. As we set specific goals, we are preparing our brains to change or create new patterns to achieve them. The focus attached to the goals can grow stronger connections between neurons, which feeds into motivation and focus; all of which boost our self-esteem, sense of autonomy and general wellbeing.

My goals prior to the first taraweeh *(prayer after isha during Ramadan)*

How I am feeling now

How I may want to refine my approach to my goals

SMALL ACTS OF KINDNESS

The first ten days (*ashra*) of Ramadan focus on mercy. A name of Allah is The Most Merciful (*Ar-Rahim*), so this becomes an opportunity to exercise humility and gratitude, as a means of attaining God's mercy, while being merciful to others.

The Prophet (PBUH) said, 'The most beloved of deeds to Allah are those that are most consistent, even if it is small.' (Bukhari). Taking small and regular steps facilitates motivation and sustainability of change. When we engage in repetitive actions, the neural pathways attached to these actions become further ingrained, highlighting the power of habit formation.

Show mercy through acts of kindness, but what would this look like for you? You could volunteer at the local *masjid* to help with *iftar* or give donations to charity, or give up your seat on your commute to work or even greet others with a smile.

What acts of kindness can I do to better my character?

_____

_____

_____

_____

How I incorporate changes to my Ramadan routine

_____

_____

_____

_____

MINDFUL EATING

As you prepare to open or break your fast, practise eating mindfully. It is preferable to pick something you can hold – a date, for example. As you move through the steps, absorb yourself and take your time. Before you begin eating the entire meal, perhaps read your *salah* and then return to the dinner table once you've prayed.

1. Just before you pick up the date, observe how it looks, noticing its texture, size and colour.

2. Now, pick up the date. Notice how it feels to touch, its texture and its weight, even as you gently roll it. As you hold the date to your nose, get a sense of the smell. If possible, open the date and observe the above.

3. Next, place the date in your mouth and let it rest on your tongue. Hold off eating for a moment and notice how it feels in your mouth. Is the texture the same as holding it in your hand? How does it taste?

4. As you begin to slowly chew your food, notice how your teeth bite into it and the texture changes. Now pay attention to the flavour and how it travels across your mouth and tongue. As you continue to chew, pay close attention to all the sensations as you eat. Think about how it was brought to your plate with gratitude. Say *Alhumdulillah* (thank you, God).

How else I can practise eating or drinking mindfully

_____

_____

_____

_____

How did I find this? What did it feel like? Did I notice anything different?

_____

_____

_____

_____

_____

SLOW AND STEADY

As humans, we are creatures of habit – both good and bad. But, as we acknowledge the holistic importance of Ramadan, this involves thinking about what we might want to abstain from and replacing it with something better and more reflective of who we want to be. However, the most important idea is to maintain the month with steady moments. Do what would be most pleasing to Him and you will be rewarded, *insha'Allah*.

Having structure for the holy month is essential, but more importantly, think about how sustainable it is. Be mindful of the intensity and the quantity of what you are doing – Ramadan is a bit of a marathon, not a sprint, where we want to reduce the risk of falling in the first *ashra*.

Make attempts to go the extra mile for Allah (SWT), but know that unrealistic expectations may have adverse effects – go gently and start with small building blocks. Having the desire to challenge ourselves or to be as productive as possible can be powerful, but it is just as important to be pragmatic.

How I can foster a consistent approach and maximize my experience this month

_____

_____

_____

_____

Health factors, urgent responsibilities, or other adjustments that I need to consider

_____

_____

_____

SLEEP WELL

During Ramadan, your body will have to adjust to the early wake-up times and eating during sundown hours. This is no easy feat, as it is a disruption to your normal routine. In the first week especially, your sleep may be deprived due to the change in eating patterns. We know that sleep is a crucial part of our wellbeing, allowing learning to embed, memories to be processed and the body to repair itself and us to feel restored. This is why we will want to factor in sleep hygiene.

There are several elements of trying to complete Ramadan with rest. Make the effort to create boundaries with each of these aspects, be it after *taraweeh* prayers or the time to wake up for *suhoor*. Good sleep hygiene will reap its rewards. What changes do you need to make to help you feel better rested throughout the month?

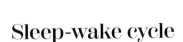

Sleep-wake cycle

Ensure that you have a consistent window of sleep, after *taraweeh* prayer and before *suhoor* (including *tahajjud* – night prayer after sleep), and then after *fajr* (morning prayer). If you notice that your energy levels dip or you are tired, assess where it may be helpful to squeeze in a power nap. Furthermore, exposure to natural light is beneficial for our circadian rhythm.

Slowing down

It is essential that you are mindful of how you are feeling and what is in store for the day/week ahead – plan your rest, prioritize tasks and pace yourself.

Sleeping conditions

The blue light emitted from our tech devices can disrupt our sleep; therefore, prior to sleeping, those stimulating screens can keep the brain awake when you need crucial wind-down time. Place your device safely away from your place of sleep to prevent the urge to see to it repeatedly. The room can be darkened, or at least at a comfortably lit setting so that your body can prepare for sleep.

Food consumption

The timing of *suhoor* can make it a challenge to follow a bedtime routine, as there are commitments to praying *isha* (night prayer) and *taraweeh*. Additionally, if you're following a special diet, do note that it's vital to adhere to that in the small window you will have to eat. Remember to avoid caffeine/stimulants late into the evening.

Healthy practices

We want to be as relaxed as possible when heading to bed. This is where activities like exercising during the day, having a routine such as a hot bath or light stretching or meditation or praying or breathing/relaxation exercises or reading, and transferring our problems onto paper (instead of taking them to bed) can help.

My sleep routine – changes or adjustments that I need to factor in and implement for myself, to help with feeling more rested

ACKNOWLEDGE THE GOOD

It can be very easy for us to overlook our deeds. What we want to be mindful of is reflecting on the positive actions that we also take as Muslims, especially the seemingly insignificant or minor acts. When we give ourselves perspective, it lifts our mood, feeds optimism, reduces stress and gives us a sense of control to frame our actions in a positive mindset.

As creatures of habit, we can extend to being mindful of the teaching of our beloved Prophet (PBUH), 'If the Day of Resurrection were established upon one of you, while he has in his hand a sapling (small plant), then let him plant it.' (Ahmad).

This can include noticing the fine details of what we do, such as reciting the *du'a* for entering your home, attending *taraweeh* at the *masjid*, helping cut the fruit for *iftar*, or even acknowledging when you take a break during a busy day or take time to contact a loved one.

The small acts or fine details in my day (either I offer, receive, or experience them) which reflect goodness or pleases the All-Mighty

_____

_____

_____

_____

_____

Daily activities I can include in my routine which mirror my Islamic values

_____

_____

_____

_____

_____

BE COMPASSIONATE

There are many benefits attached to being connected to fellow humans. When we connect, happiness increases and depression reduces and in the long-term it can make us more resilient and able to cope with stress more easily.

There are three types of: giving (offering support and care to others), receiving (accepting care and support when finding it difficult) and inner (giving compassion to ourselves when suffering). It is common that we can have high expectations and standards for ourselves, and when they are not met, how are we left feeling? This can include not reaching certain goals or fulfilling things which we set for ourselves. Notice when you think harshly about your actions and think about how you can be more compassionate to yourself and others.

'My servants who have transgressed against their souls! Do not lose hope in Allah's mercy, for Allah certainly forgives all sins. He is indeed the All-Forgiving, Most Merciful.' (Qur'an, 39:53). Notice your inner critic, and practise speaking compassionately to yourself. Think about how you would speak, and the kind of tone and language you will use.

I can speak kindly to myself by

_____

_____

_____

_____

_____

I can be compassionate towards others by

_____

_____

_____

_____

_____

FIND TIME FOR FORGIVENESS

The second *ashra* of Ramadan focus on forgiveness. One of the ninety-nine names of Allah (SWT) is The Oft Forgiving (*Ar-Rahman*). Therefore, seek His forgiveness, while forgiving others. Making *du'a* before you open your fast is one of the best times, as The Prophet (PBUH) said: 'Whatever is prayed for at the time of breaking the fast is granted and never refused.' (Tirmidhi).

People who tend to be more forgiving often experience more satisfaction and contentment, as well as improved mental health, such as reduced symptoms of depression or anxiety. This is because holding onto angry feelings maintains the cycle of negative thoughts and emotions, which can affect our wellbeing. Ask for forgiveness and have the power of forgiveness.

How can I forgive and be forgiven? One example is to read istighfar (seeking forgiveness) on a tasbih.

How I can attain God's mercy and forgiveness

How I can forgive others

GROUND YOURSELF

Ramadan is a month for creating profound memories. It can also trigger difficult memories for some people. Perhaps you have lost a loved one, or in the past found the month to be challenging. This can linger and derail our mood. This practice is an opportunity to anchor ourselves when feeling overwhelmed and use our senses to respond with mindfulness and acceptance. Prepare to take time out for yourself to recuperate from an episode of negative thinking.

1. Acknowledge your inner experiences – whatever you are experiencing, put it into words (silently or loudly), e.g. 'I am feeling anger' or 'I notice a difficult memory'.

2. Come back to your body – regain control by returning to the present and through movement, e.g. stretch, slow your breathing, stand up or change your posture.

3. Engage with the world – expand your awareness by using your senses and noticing where you are, what you are doing, what you can see, touch, hear, smell and taste.

How I can practise this exercise to ground myself in situations of feeling overwhelmed

_____

_____

_____

_____

_____

_____

How I felt before and afterwards

_____

_____

_____

_____

_____

_____

BE CHARITABLE

As Muslims, charity (*zakat*) is one of the five pillars. This functions as a huge act of worship, where The Prophet (PBUH) said, 'The best charity is that given in Ramadan' (Bukhari and Muslim) and 'The believer's shade on the Day of Resurrection will be their charity.' (Tirmidhi).

Charitable actions have both physical and mental health benefits, as they increase happiness and longevity. The results can be profound, such as reducing your stress as you will have a greater sense of purpose in line with Islamic values. There is a strengthening of our connection to others and it triggers the release of oxytocin.

There are many ways to be charitable, e.g. volunteering in any capacity, giving time to community groups, donating to charity, feeding the birds in your garden, or even helping to prepare for *iftar*.

How I can offer charity and/or connect with my community

_____

_____

_____

_____

_____

_____

_____

_____

POSITIVE AFFIRMATIONS

Have you ever given yourself a pep talk? That's completely normal, to vocalize your internal monologue or even silently whisper a *du'a*. Self-talk is a fundamental pillar in our cognitive development and general wellbeing. Your inner voice impacts all aspects of your life, from your belief system to the relationships you nurture, to the purpose and direction of your life, as well as how you navigate your every day.

Think about how you can practise connecting positive affirmations to Allah (SWT) and cultivate compassionate self-talk with yourself, to strengthen your self-belief and resilience. During Ramadan, affirmations of Allah (SWT) instil contentment and stillness within us and bring us closer to Him.

My morning affirmations

_____

_____

_____

_____

_____

_____

Du'as that I can use in times of stress

_____

_____

_____

_____

_____

_____

BREATHE DEEPLY

Breathwork is when we intentionally control how we breathe to experience a sense of tranquillity. This is because when we feel anxious or stressed, we may notice that our breathing becomes short and shallow, and we stiffen or tighten around the shoulders and chest. If we only breathe into the top regions of the lungs, we restrict airflow in the body, and this can create discomfort. Deep breathing can help improve focus, as we are more mindful of our thoughts and feelings, allowing us to be more present.

1. Gently inhale through your nose, allowing air to flow to the bottom of your belly and let it fully expand.

2. Noticing the expansion of your stomach, feel the rise in your chest and shoulders. If you can, hold your breath for a few seconds.

3. Slowly exhale through your mouth, releasing air from your diaphragm region in order to let the body and shoulders fully relax.

4. You will notice your heart rate slow down, and if you repeat this a few times, it can help to ground you when things feel overwhelming.

Ways I can practise deep breathing (it can be after praying your salah, or during a walk)

_____

_____

_____

_____

How did you find this? Did you notice anything different?

_____

_____

_____

_____

_____

_____

_____

THE POWER OF VISUALIZATION

The Qur'an is exemplary for its storytelling, filled with many parables. 'In their stories there is truly a lesson for people of reason. This message cannot be a fabrication, rather (it is) a confirmation of previous revelation, a detailed explanation of all things, a guide, and a mercy for people of faith.' (Qur'an, 12:111). As humans, we know how powerful imagery can be and this is something we can cultivate during the holy month.

1. Visualizing God's power – being mindful of the capabilities He possesses which are beyond our comprehension. The story of Jonah (peace be upon him) is one example.

2. Visualizing our goals vs God's plan – we aspire and are driven towards attaining our goals, so being aware of His willingness to accept our *du'as* will only fuel our desire to connect with Him.

3. Visualizing the world and humanity – stories in the Qur'an can offer perspective on how the world can be, reminding us to be mindful and view it with realism and humility.

Goals to visualize for myself during Ramadan and beyond

_____

_____

_____

_____

_____

How did I find giving this a go? What wisdom can/do I derive from the plans He bestows upon us?

_____

_____

_____

_____

_____

GO SLOWLY AND PRIORITIZE

Life is extremely busy and even more so when there are specific occasions, such as our religious festivals or the holy month of Ramadan. This is where we will have many things planned for ourselves and perhaps added responsibilities or commitments, on top of those that already exist.

This is a chance for us to slow down, conserve our energy and ensure that our goals for the holy month are met. A time management matrix can help us focus on tasks that ought to be prioritized, allowing us to give more of our devotion to what is important.

How can I take steps towards mindfully prioritizing my tasks?

	Urgent	**Not urgent**
Important	Do the task	Plan the task for later
Not important	Delegate the task to someone	Remove it

How did I find taking this approach?

_____

_____

THE REMAINING DAYS
OF RAMADAN

The last *ashra* of Ramadan focus on purifying the soul and being the best Muslim we can be. This period is when we ought to utilize the power of prayer to cleanse our souls and devote ourselves entirely to the All-Mighty.

It is a period that includes *Laylatul Qadr*, the night 'better than a thousand months' (Qur'an, 97:3). It's in this special night that the very first verses of the Qur'an were bestowed upon The Prophet Muhammad (PBUH): 'Whoever prays on *Laylatul Qadr* out of faith and sincerity, shall have all their past sins forgiven.' (Bukhari and Muslim).

It is encouraged to pray for every night in the last *ashra* as it is not set what date this precious night may fall on. The Prophet Muhammad (PBUH) said, 'Seek it in the last ten days, on the off nights.' (Bukhari and Muslim).

There are many ways to enact good deeds as a Muslim, e.g. through performing charity, performing *ibaadah* or worship (praying *salah*, reading the Qur'an, making *dhikr*, praying *du'a*) as well as undertaking *itikaaf* (the Islamic practice of staying in a mosque for a night and devoting your entire time to *ibaadah*).

How I can spend the remaining days of Ramadan

LABELLING EMOTIONS

Mindfully noticing and labelling your emotions as they surface can help reduce the effects of stress and anxiety. Throughout an average day we have many thoughts, some which are fleeting, others which are more intense and enduring. This is where, by naming emotions as they surface, the part of our brain responsible for thought is reactivated, inherently soothing the area of the brain involved in creating the stress response.

During Ramadan, finding time to sit with our thoughts is a powerful tool. Whether it's labelling the changes that come with fasting, or difficult interactions with others, naming our emotions can help to facilitate a healthy distance between yourself and what it is that evokes such a strong impulse within you. It is by resisting the urge to react immediately and instead taking a breather to pause, we can mindfully respond in a manner which pleases Him.

The moment you notice your body evoking a strong emotional response, you can try the following:

1. Notice what you're feeling, i.e. name the emotion in your head, and inhale slowly and deeply (while closing your eyes).

2. Recognize with compassion why this situation creates such a response – exhale slowly and allow the breathing to dissipate the stress.

3. Name out loud what it is you are feeling.

4. Notice your body becoming more relaxed and slowly calming down as you both inhale and exhale.

5. Do this until you feel satisfied to respond or are ready to open your eyes.

What I noticed labelling
my emotions and how I found this

_____

_____

_____

_____

_____

_____

_____

_____

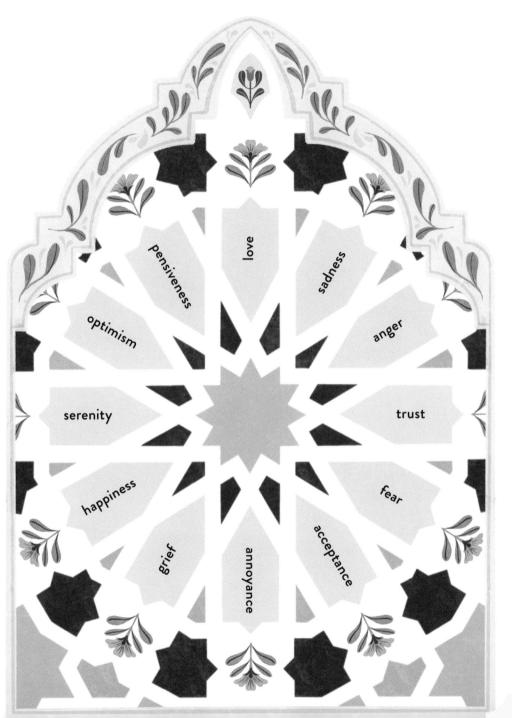

DIFFUSING THOUGHTS

Humans are renowned for storytelling. This includes the stories we tell ourselves. More significantly, how we relate to these stories can influence our sense of self and our connection with others. If we are fused to our thoughts, we tend to believe them as absolute, which can spill into unhelpful behaviours. This attachment between our thoughts and feelings can make it difficult to separate our reality from our personal experience over time.

Just because it is the holy month, it does not mean that we cannot experience difficulties with our thoughts and feelings. It's important to take gentle steps towards recognizing negative thoughts for what they are. This helps us act in accordance with our Islamic values and in a manner which pleases Allah (SWT). Diffusing our thoughts can help us to stay present and increase flexibility with our perspective, reduce the influence of our thoughts and how much we allow them to define us.

*Ways I can become more mindful of my thoughts
and diffuse my attachment to them*

How did I find this? Did I notice anything different?

EID UL-FITR AND GIVING THANKS

Eid ul-Fitr is the celebration at the end of Ramadan. After a month of fasting, prayers, supplications and good deeds, Muslims bid farewell to the spiritually galvanizing month and welcome festivities with loved ones.

Before attending the communal prayer at the *masjid*, you will want to make sure that you have made *fitrana* (charity at the end of Ramadan) in advance. This is to ensure that those in need have food in time for Eid. As The Prophet (PBUH) said, 'It acts as a means of purifying the fasting person from indecent words or actions.' (Abu Dawud and Ibn Majah).

My Eid Checklist

- Morning *ghusl* (bathing/showering) for Eid *salah*

- Wear new clothes

- Eat something sweet before leaving the home

- Attend *masjid* early to recite *takbeerat* (praising God with gratitude) and listen to the *khutbah* (sermon) from the imam

- [ ] Pray two *rakat* (unit of prayer) of *tahiyyat al-masjid* (*sunnah* prayer) upon entering and greeting the *masjid*

- [ ] Attend Eid ul-Fitr *salah*

- [ ] Exchange Eid greetings with friends, family members and local community members of all ages

- [ ] Take a different route to and from the *masjid*

My plans to celebrate Eid ul-Fitr will include

_____

_____

_____

_____

_____

_____

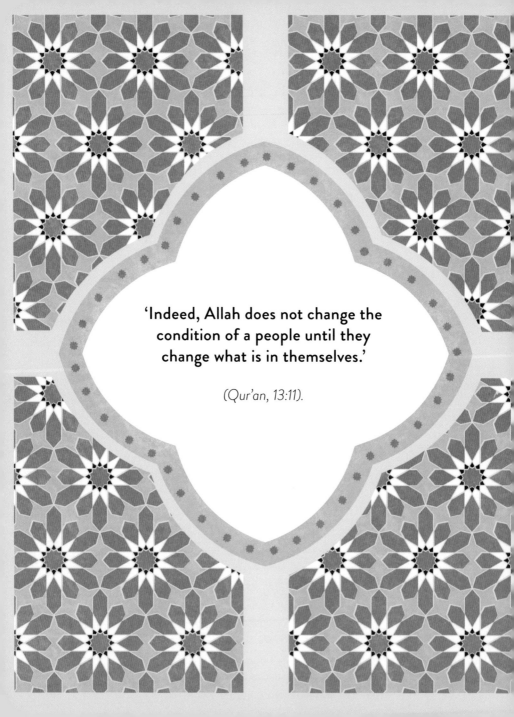

'Indeed, Allah does not change the condition of a people until they change what is in themselves.'

(Qur'an, 13:11).

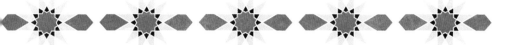

BEYOND RAMADAN

Although we are now at the end of the beautiful month, this is just the beginning. How can you review what you have done and apply the principles of our *deen* to our daily lives? This section will explore avenues of refining and fortifying the new, healthier habits into the rest of our year. Be mindful that change is a journey and one that has its fair share of turbulence. This is where being conscious of and placing our trust in Him allows us to focus on what we can control, to be as present in the moment as possible and work towards a life with meaning.

The Prophet (PBUH) narrated: 'Allah said, "O son of Adam, stand for Me, and I will walk to you. Walk to Me, and I will come running to you".' (Ahmad). How can you become empowered to strengthen your *deen*?

GROWTH MINDSET

A crucial part of Ramadan is taking steps towards self-development and personal growth (*tazkiyah*). Internal or external expectations can place great pressure on making you believe that anything short of perfection is unacceptable. However, The Prophet (PBUH) stated: 'All children of Adam are sinners, and the best of those who sin is those who repent.' (Tirmidhi). This demonstrates the value of progress, as mistakes and failures are a fact of life.

Learning from experiences helps to foster psychological flexibility. Ramadan is a landscape for us to practise our *deen* in a meaningful manner and utilize the benefits of the month in other aspects of our life.

Ask yourself – how was Ramadan this year? What did I do to remember Allah (SWT)? How can I continue to take this forward? What will I do different next year?

What Ramadan has meant to me

_____

_____

_____

_____

_____

_____

_____

_____

_____

_____

EVERYDAY GRATITUDE

As Ramadan ends, we enter *Shawwal* (the tenth month of the Islamic calendar) – this is a good opportunity to make up for the fasts which were missed. We often gravitate to viewing our lives and experiences from a lens of negativity. The Prophet (PBUH) said: 'Look at those who are lower than you and do not look at those who are higher than you, lest you belittle the favours Allah conferred upon you.' (Muslim).

There are numerous benefits of gratitude, such as a reduced desire for material gains, and increased physical health and wellbeing. This is a core component of faith: recognizing the good which we experience, in any or every aspect possible, and exemplifying it through our actions.

What I can do to demonstrate gratitude

DEEP PATIENCE

'We will certainly test you with a touch of fear, hunger, loss of wealth, lives and fruits, but give glad tidings to the patient, who, when afflicted by calamity, say, "Indeed, to Allah we belong and to Him we will return."' (Qur'an, 2:155-156).

Experiencing hardship is part of what makes us human. All of us will endure trials and tribulations in this life. It is through *taqwa* and *tawakkul* that we maintain patience (*sabr*), and a firm belief in His plan.

By being mindful of this, we can actively navigate stress or strong emotions in a manner which is pleasing to Him and facilitates our ability to regulate ourselves – away from impulsivity or agitation. The Prophet (PBUH) said, 'Nothing afflicts a Muslim of hardship, nor illness, nor anxiety, nor sorrow, nor harm, nor distress, nor even the pricking of a thorn, but that Allah will expiate his sins by it.' (Bukhari).

How I can perceive hardship with patience, tawakkul and mindfulness

IMMERSE YOURSELF

You can't buy back time that has already passed, which makes it ever more important to spend it wisely and in a way that is consistent with what you feel will bring contentment to you. This includes how you remember Allah (SWT) and with whom you share your company.

The Prophet Muhammad (PBUH) was asked about whose company was best, and he responded with, 'One whose appearance reminds you of God, and whose speech increases you in knowledge, and whose actions remind you of the hereafter.' (Al-Muhasibi).

The environment we find ourselves in influences us heavily and in many ways. Think about places that enable you to reflect and feel at peace, whether that is with close friends or family, or perhaps a location (such as the holy city of Makkah) that is special to you.

Environments that are important to me

_____

_____

_____

_____

_____

How I can ensure they become part of my life more regularly

_____

_____

_____

_____

SELF-AWARENESS

The ability to be self-aware revolves around being able to monitor our states mindfully and pay attention to how experiences can affect us, with honesty and compassion, and without judgement. This is the accumulation of the self-reflection you have undertaken and choices you have then made. It is the art of knowing yourself.

It is also a predictor of quality of life, which can aid our decision making: both in the *dunya* and *akhirah*.

We are likely to have experienced many different emotions during the holy month, but how conscious and observant were we? Make a note of what stands out for you and write down details of what happened and how it made you feel. What did you do to cope? How does it shape what you will do in life moving forward?

My thoughts and feelings about my Ramadan

HEALTHY HABITS

After Ramadan ends, the spiritual gardening you have done will begin to harvest changes – perhaps ones which you had envisaged or perhaps not even considered. As you have developed new, healthier habits, your brain's neuroplasticity – the ability to adapt and change according to purpose and drive and discipline – will be changing as well.

You may find that your mood and wellbeing increases, as you have taken time to tend to the areas (spiritual, psychological, physical and emotional) which have a profound impact on the fabric of your existence as a Muslim.

The Messenger (PBUH) narrated, 'There are two blessings in which many people incur loss. (They are) health and free time (for doing good).' (Bukhari). Through being mindful of what we are doing and the purpose behind each action, whether aligning with our values or to please Him, there is a strengthening of our humanity and cause as a Muslim.

What practices I liked or found helpful throughout the holy month

_____

_____

_____

_____

_____

_____

What I can introduce or continue to do, to strengthen my healthy habits

_____

_____

_____

_____

YOUR NEW GOALS

Within Islam, life is not confined to the limitations of this present world. This is where we view our existence across the planes of the *dunya* and *akhirah* – our decisions are influenced to benefit both arenas, with the primary focus being on the next life.

The Prophet (PBUH) said, 'The strong believer is more beloved to Allah than the weak believer, but there is goodness in both of them. Be eager for what benefits you, seek help from Allah, and do not be frustrated. If something befalls you, then do not say, "if only I had done something else". Rather, say, "Allah has decreed what He wills". Verily, the phrase "if only" opens the way for the work of Satan.' (Muslim).

As Ramadan comes to an end, it can be worthwhile reflecting on what you would like to continue that can be of benefit to strengthening your *deen*. What did you find beneficial, for this life and the hereafter? What do you want to continue? What steps are you taking in preparation for the *akhirah*?

My Ramadan reflections going forward

About the Author

Humza Khan is an accredited psychotherapist (BABCP) who works within primary care adult mental health in the NHS. He graduated from King's College London and Royal Holloway University, specializing in cognitive behavioural psychotherapy and delivering evidence-based treatment. He also works as a teacher and guest lecturer at world famous institutions across the UK, such as University College London and University of Exeter. He has a strong interest in mental health and is experienced in working with a broad range of presentation and difficulties, such as depression and anxiety-based disorders. This extends to the inextricable link between Islam and psychology. He has a passion for using an integrated framework and the third-wave approaches of CFT (compassion focused therapy), ACT (acceptance and commitment), and Mindfulness, as well as including the application of faith. Humza was born in London to Pakistani parents, as a second-generation migrant.

About the Illustrators

Lione and Sheikh is a small UK-based business driven by passion and creativity. The company was founded by Hope Lione and Amirah Sheikh in 2021, two best friends turned business partners who wanted to combine their design styles to create a range of decorative stationery, from beautifully illustrated greeting cards to hand-printed artworks, which sell online and in-store through many retailers around the world.